# The Inmate's Guide to Success As an Author

## How to Win at the Marketing Game from Prison

Francis Raemond

Cadmus Publishing
www.cadmuspublishing.com

Copyright © 2022 Francis Raemond

Cover art by Sean McCord

Published by Cadmus Publishing
www.cadmuspublishing.com
Port Angeles, WA

ISBN: 978-1-63751-362-0

All rights reserved. Copyright under Berne Copyright Convention, Universal Copyright Convention, and Pan-American Copyright Convention. No part of this book may be reproduced, stored in a retrieval system, or transmitted in any form, or by any means, electronic, mechanical, photocopying, recording or otherwise, without prior permission of the author.

# Table of Contents

Introduction. . . . . . . . . . . . . . . . . . . . . 1
Disclaimer. . . . . . . . . . . . . . . . . . . . . . 3
**Part I: The Basics** . . . . . . . . . . . . . . . . **5**
Chapter 1: Do I Really Need To Do This? . . . . . . . . 6
Chapter 2: Who The Hell Am I To Tell You How To Market Your Book? . . . . . . . . . . . . . . . . 10
Chapter 3: Understanding Some Basic Ideas . . . . . . . 15
Chapter 4: Where To Start? . . . . . . . . . . . . . . 19
Chapter 5: Who Are You Writing For? . . . . . . . . . 21
Chapter 6: Read More Books . . . . . . . . . . . . . 24
Chapter 7: Read Even More Books. . . . . . . . . . . 26
**Part II: Before You Publish…** . . . . . . . . . . . **28**
Chapter 8: Revise! . . . . . . . . . . . . . . . . . . 29
Chapter 9: Beta Readers! . . . . . . . . . . . . . . . 31
Chapter 10: Professional Edit. . . . . . . . . . . . . 34
Chapter 11: Cover! . . . . . . . . . . . . . . . . . 38
Chapter 12: Title! . . . . . . . . . . . . . . . . . . 41
Chapter 13: Layout . . . . . . . . . . . . . . . . . 43
Chapter 14: Pricing! . . . . . . . . . . . . . . . . . 45
Chapter 15: Metadata . . . . . . . . . . . . . . . . 48
**Part III: Actual Marketing Stuff** . . . . . . . . . . **54**
Chapter 16: Introduction: Reprise . . . . . . . . . . . 55
Chapter 17: Letter Writing . . . . . . . . . . . . . . 57
Chapter 18: Word Of Mouth . . . . . . . . . . . . . 63
Chapter 19: Submitting Articles . . . . . . . . . . . . 65
Chapter 20: Interviews . . . . . . . . . . . . . . . . 68

Chapter 21: Brick & Mortar. . . . . . . . . . . . . . . . . 71
Chapter 22: Keep Copies Handy . . . . . . . . . . . . . . 74
Chapter 23: Magazine/Newspaper Ads . . . . . . . . . 76
Chapter 24: Online Advertising. . . . . . . . . . . . . . . 79
Chapter 25: Press Release . . . . . . . . . . . . . . . . . . 83
Chapter 26: Leveraging The Fact Of Your Incarceration; Also, Son Of Sam Laws . . . . . . . . . . . . . . . . . . . . . 85
Chapter 27: Social Media . . . . . . . . . . . . . . . . . . 88
Chapter 28: Author Webpage . . . . . . . . . . . . . . . . 92
Chapter 29: Write More Books . . . . . . . . . . . . . . 94
Chapter 30: Audiobooks . . . . . . . . . . . . . . . . . . . 97
Chapter 31: Book Reviews . . . . . . . . . . . . . . . . . 99
Afterward . . . . . . . . . . . . . . . . . . . . . . . . . . . .103
Appendix A: Resources . . . . . . . . . . . . . . . . . . .105
Appendix B: Sample Press Releases . . . . . . . . . .110
Appendix C: About the Author. . . . . . . . . . . . . .114

## Introduction

So, you wrote a book. It took some time, a lot of work, and you figured out how to get it published, which was probably not easy either. Now it's time to sit back, and let those sweet, sweet royalties roll in.

Ha! You WISH you had the hard part behind you! The truth is most authors find that marketing their book is as hard or *harder* than writing it. At least with writing the book, it is something that comes from you. It's your creation, your rules. It is done how you want it to be done. But with marketing... well, some things will work and some won't, and it isn't up to you which ones will or won't. In fact, what even ARE your options for how to market the book?

And let's add to the difficulty. Let's do it all while locked up. Where you really can't rely on anything, or anyone. Well, you have one thing you can rely on, friend – and that's me. I'm here to guide you through some of the most popular and successful options you have available to you for marketing your book. And you better believe you need to market it: *If people don't know it exists, they can't buy it.*

But it's not all doom and gloom. There is a light at the end of the tunnel. A pot of gold at the end of the rainbow: You CAN do it. With the tools you have at your disposal – and this book in your hand – it is possible to make incredible sales numbers: high enough even to rival national best sellers. It won't happen for everybody, and there are a lot of factors that will contribute to how successful you are, but it

CAN be you. Nobody but yourself can stop you from making a comfortable income from your writing.

And think of this: you have an advantage. People on the outside have to deal with 9 to 5 jobs, bills, groceries, shopping, vacation, family... all that stuff that you miss out on. But what they don't have, because of all these things, is a lot of time on their hands. This is where your advantage lies. With all the time you have right now, you can be building a successful library of your own works. And here's lesson number one (which we'll dive into more, later in the book): The more you write, the more you'll sell. But let's get started!

## Disclaimer

This book is for educational purposes. While not presented as a comprehensive course in marketing, it is written in good faith and with many years of experience – both personal and observational. However, as is stated later, no marketing plan is a sure thing. It is up to the reader to perform any additional research they deem necessary before taking any steps and spending any money in the marketing of their book. The ideas, opinions, and options included herein do not guarantee high sales and success – indeed, there is nothing in life that can truly carry that guarantee. Neither the author nor the publisher are liable for any losses suffered through your marketing tactics. We are also not liable for any successes, but would love to hear about them from you!

In short: read, learn, further your education as you see fit, and do what works best for you based on your own decisions. Keep this book handy and reference back to it as you continue to work through your own marketing strategy; with your knowledge of what you want and what resources you have, this work will help guide you towards the success of your own book.

# FRANCIS RAEMOND

# Part I

# The Basics

## Chapter 1

## Do I Really Need To Do This?

The short answer is, "Yes."

The long answer is still "Yes," just with a lot more words.

As I stated in the Introduction (right near the middle of it – you did read that, right?), people can't buy your book if they don't know it exists. That one sentence is very important, so let's try it again, with feeling:

**PEOPLE CAN'T BUY YOUR BOOK IF THEY DON'T KNOW IT EXISTS!**

I mean, it's simple logic, right? But it seems that too many authors forget this basic fact. "Well, the book is on Amazon. It's got its genres listed, so when people look for [my genre] they'll find my book!" Or maybe even, "I have an author webpage, so when people see that, they'll find the book from there."

I'm sorry, but neither of those things are just going to happen. There are literally millions of books out there, and likely hundreds of thousands in your genre alone. The odds of just stumbling onto yours are so slim as to be hardly worth mentioning. The same, of course, goes for any website you may have, or whatever social media presence you've set up to promote yourself and/or your book.

That's not to say that you should just give up hope, or even that you should forego having a social media presence or a website – those are both excellent assets which we will be addressing later.

But you need more. And you do have options, even in your position. Your options will vary widely based on the resources you have available to you – both in personnel and money. Some things are cheap or free but need people to put forth the time to do them. Some are expensive but require less personal time, or at least are easily hired out. If you have neither time nor money there is very little you can do.

This is where many people out here in the streets run into trouble: we're working our jobs, 40 hours or more every week and dealing with family and social lives and everything else that takes up our time, leaving us with very little downtime. But often those same people also have very little income to devote to their marketing, or just don't feel the need to put their precious funds to work for their book.

As you can see – you've already got one strong advantage over the authors out here in the 'real world': you have time. It's true that many of you may have a prison job that takes up some of your time, and you have your social activities as well, maybe even a side hustle. But when it comes down to it, you don't need to worry about housing, food, or clothing. You can reduce your social activities easily. There are so many ways in which you simply have significantly more time on your hands than the people out here. Use it. You don't have many advantages where you are, but that one – time – you do have. Make sure to use it wisely. Now, if you have some funding or a good support network, or maybe even associates who want to invest in you and your book, then you have a bit of cash as well. You truly are well positioned to make an impact in the literary world. So do it.

Marketing is not a one time thing, either. You can't just tell someone about your book (either by directly speaking to them about it or by doing some other form of marketing) and expect that they will go out and buy it right now. Think about Coca Cola. You know what Coke is, right? In fact, do you know anyone that does NOT know what it is? And yet you still see their ads on TV, hear them on the radio, and see them in many magazines and newspapers. Why is that? Who do they think doesn't know about them?

So, they're not trying to make you aware that they exist... but then, what *are* they doing? I'll tell you: Repetition. If something isn't in your head at the right time, the right moment... you'll forget about it when you could be buying it. Or maybe, having it in your head right now means that you're going to actually go forth with the express intent of purchasing a bottle of brown, sugary beverage. Repetition is a key component of successful marketing, and those big brands know it. And now, so do you. Or at least the basic fact that it's a thing. We'll get into it more, later.

All this to say: Yes, you really need to market your book. Long answer.

## Chapter 2

## Who The Hell Am I To Tell You How To Market Your Book?

Good question. But fear not, I have the background to provide you with the relevant information.

First, I literally wrote the book on marketing from prison (which should be obvious, as you're reading it right now). So clearly I know what I'm talking about. Yeah, I know: bad joke.

The reality of it is, while I may not have had the misfortune to be in prison, or to have published a book from there, I have been working with incarcerated authors for many years. I've seen some of the impressive work that comes out of prisons, and I've also seen all too often how it fails to reach the audience it deserves simply because the author didn't know enough about how to market their book. Now, there are a plethora of marketing books out there, and I've recommended many of them to my clients in the past. But none of them are targeted specifically to inmates. And they should be. As a free man I can go online and find a ton of resources, tips, recommendations, and more on how to market my book. I can find consultants and companies willing to do it all for me, for a price. I don't actually need 349 books telling me the same things in different ways. This is not to say that I don't have a couple of them sitting on my shelf – a web page will never beat out a physical book for me. But an incarcerated author doesn't have these resources. From prison, one cannot simply hop on the internet, or find a phone number for a company or expert to handle this stuff for them.

And this is distressing because there should be a lot more best-sellers coming from inmates. Why? Because who else has such a great opportunity to get their career as a writer kick-started? I mentioned this earlier, in my introduction: who else has the advantage of lots of time with few of the day-to-day concerns of someone on the outside? I have worked with inmates who have upwards of FIFTY books already written, and are just trying to figure out how to get them out into the world! In my career in the publishing industry I have seen far too many books either not get published at all, or which fail to perform in the market just because they were written by an inmate without the resources or the knowledge to make it all happen.

But I digress. As I was saying, I have worked with inmates a lot throughout my career. And I'm very familiar with the restrictions you have and the hurdles you face; I'm also familiar with what resources you may have available to overcome those hurdles.

On the other side of things, I have made a successful career in the industry – as mentioned, I've been working in publishing – largely on the marketing side of things – for many years and have been happy to see authors succeed and make a career out of it.

In particular I consult for a company, Cadmus Publishing (the very publishers who are releasing this book), which has really stepped up to the plate in their support of incarcerated authors. In fact, if you are not already working with them, it is recommended that you drop them a line to see what they can do for you – many of the options in this book are services they can provide or help you with. And most importantly, they work with incarcerated authors: accepting phone calls, snail mail, and many prison email systems. That alone sets them apart (for the incarcerated author) from most other publishing services out there.

There are also a good number of books out there – written by inmates like yourself – that talk about how to write a book from prison. How to get it published. What worked for them. What didn't work. Many of those books are very good: I've read at least a dozen of them myself over the years in the course of doing my job and helping my clients get the most out of their work.

However, most of those are aimed strictly at writing and publishing urban novels. Some of them have a couple of marketing tips. Some of them have some very good advice. Excellent advice, I would go so far as to say. But they have their limitations. Some of them have only one or two ideas. Some of them require a large, very helpful network of people on the outside. Some of them are specifically for only one type of book.

This book you hold in your hands is my attempt to fill in the gaps left by each of those other books – the general marketing books, the inmate-written books on writing, etc. Look, if you want to learn how to write a great urban novel then this isn't the book for you. If you just want to know how to get your book published from prison, this isn't the book for you (though I've mentioned – and will mention – a couple companies that can help you get those things done).

As I write this book for you, dear reader/author, I assume *you* have a written a great book. *You* already know you've written a great book; or maybe you're ready to do so – and I will also add that you did well in getting and reading this book before you start writing your own! I also assume you have a way to get it published (but if you don't, I will touch on this and other related topics in the chapters to follow).

I assume all of this because *this* book is here to help you get rich from *your* book. I am going to tell you – as a marketing professional who has been working with incarcerated authors for years – what options you have for getting your book into as many readers' hands as possible and start bringing in those stacks and start pulling those dollars. It's time for you to max out your store limit. It's time for you to make all the calls you want. It's time for you to send some money home to your family. You CAN make a truckload of cash with your book from where you sit right now. And I've got the experience, skills, training, and knowledge to get you there. The material in these pages is gold. These options *work*. I've seen them work. I've *made* them work. For people just like you. In your exact circumstances. I've even seen authors take their books to their parole hearings, or to their judge, with their royalty statements, proving that they can make it on the outside without resorting to criminal enterprise again.

And it doesn't matter what you're in for. It doesn't matter whether you're male or female. It doesn't matter how long you're down for – or even if you *have* an out-date. What matters is that you've got a story to tell, and it deserves to be told, and the people are going to love it. You can do this.

From
Right
Where
You
Sit.

Chapter 3

# Understanding Some Basic Ideas

It is said that: "50% of all marketing works. But no one knows which 50%."

What is marketing? Well, you can break it down into three discrete styles:

**Publicity**: This is anything that draws attention to you as the author, or to your book. If you appear in the news for any reason, you could view that as publicity. Did you get a radio interview? Publicity. Did someone write an article about you? Publicity. One way to look at it is that if you didn't pay for it directly, it's publicity. This is what was meant with that old phrase, "There's no such thing as bad publicity."

**Promotion**: Anything that promotes your book, from bookmarks to posters to free hat giveaways.

**Advertisement**: Paid advertisements in books, magazines, or the internet.

These are my own definitions and an easy way to categorize different types of marketing. Some ideas in here will straddle a couple of these categories. Some ideas might be hard to squeeze into any one category and will have a different feel from anything else. But keeping these concepts in mind can help you come up with your own ideas, and also help you to keep your head on straight as you read up on the concepts and ideas presented within here.

A big question I hear a lot is, "How much money can I expect to make from my book?" The answer is… No one really knows. There is truthfully no way to tell. The things that dictate how successful a book will be are so widely varied, so impossible to quantify, and so completely unpredictable, that there is no one in the industry that can say with any certainty which books will succeed and which will fail. This is why now-famous authors have had their books rejected from major publishers dozens of times before they finally found one to take a chance on them. Steven King, for example, submitted his first books dozens of times before a publisher was willing to take a chance on him. The Harry Potter books were rejected by 12 major publishers before being accepted. (One has to assume someone lost his job over these dismissals!) But this same unpredictability is also why some books published by major book publishers fail to do so much as break even. There is just no way to tell.

However, as mentioned before – No one can buy your book if they don't know it exists (are you getting tired of this mantra yet?). That's where we are now – no one knows your book exists. That is why you need to read this, cover to cover, and maybe a couple more books as well... and then start doing *something*. Pick and choose what strategies you think will work best for you. And don't be disheartened if you don't notice an immediate rush of sales. Sometimes, it takes some time to really break into your stride. Sometimes it takes a lot of failures before you can succeed. The key is to keep trying. Persistence.

I'm going to be referencing a lot of resources in this book. I can't cover all of them in here; and for many of you it wouldn't matter – since they are often found online, or may not accept incarcerated clients, etc. In addition, these resources can come and go. New ones appear, old ones vanish.

To account for this you can find all of the sources mentioned in this book, and others that I didn't feel the need to include, and still others that appear after this book is in print, on my website. They will be in a printer-friendly format, so you can have your people on the outside go there and print off the page to send to you. You can find my website at: www.PrisonBookMarketing.com.

There's going to be a lot of stuff I *don't* cover. Things like how to find the best keywords by following some specific methods on the internet. There are a lot of technically complex things that can be done by people who have full access to the internet and other resources out here beyond the walls. However, this book is not for those people. There are plenty of other books that tell you how to do those things. And, if you have people (whether it's people you hire or friends/family) that can do them, then I *strongly* recommend you pick up another marketing book (in addition to this awesome one, obviously) and get some of those methods working for you, as well. And realize that you are among the very fortunate, very few.

Generally, I have to assume you have at least some small amount of outside help – it's pretty much necessary in order to have published your book in the first place.

Finally, *read this entire book.* Not just because I like to hear myself talk, but even sections you may think aren't relevant to you might be. There may even be a tidbit of useful information I threw in there that is VERY relevant to you, even though the rest of the section may not be. Plus, reading the ideas and options here may lead to some amazing ideas of your own. Or perhaps you'll be inspired to pursue an idea you had thought of and dismissed as out of your reach or not worth the hassle… but that will turn out working magic for you. If there's one thing I've learned it's that people in prison can be very resourceful and come up with ways to do things others may not have realized would be possible given the circumstances.

## Chapter 4

## Where To Start?

Really, before you even publish! This concept will lead us into the next few chapters, where we will go over a few ideas in greater depth. The overall thing you need to take away from these following chapters is that your book should be as good as possible in every way. Great marketing will draw people to the book – but if the book itself is a disappointment, the people will make it known. They won't tell friends or family about it, they may even tell people to avoid it. Bad reviews on your book can kill its chances before a reader even buys it.

Conversely, readers who like the book are more likely to convince friends, family, even complete strangers, to pick up a copy for themselves. Not only that, but there are other aspects of your book that must be decided on before it is published that absolutely must be optimized if you wish to draw people to buy it once your potential reading public has found it.

These are all issues that can be easily avoided, and even turned to your advantage – and we'll get to those, starting in just a few chapters. Be patient, though: let's look at a couple more things before you publish that can give you a jumpstart on selling lots of books…

Chapter 5

# Who Are You Writing For?

There's a concept: *writing for yourself vs. writing for others*. Neither option is inherently bad. They are simply different approaches to writing.

***Writing for yourself*** basically means that you are writing the book that *you* want to write. This could be anything, but is most commonly fiction or a memoir. You are not tailoring your writing just to what is popular and selling well on the general market, but writing the book you enjoy, or getting your own story out there.

This is a great approach and is what most first-time authors will do. And of course the old expression, "Write what you know" applies here. You are writing the book that you enjoy, feel comfortable with, and understand well.

The advantages to this method are numerous, but a couple significant points are:

1) Writing for yourself is fun. You are writing the story that you want to hear or telling people about the interesting events in your own life. This is a comfortable zone for you; it often doesn't even feel like work when you are doing it!

2) Writing for yourself is generally going to be 'writing what you know', and that makes it easier. You don't have to do as much research. You don't have to read a lot of other books you otherwise may not have, just to understand how they are typically written.

Writing for yourself often means that you are going to write a better book. For the very reasons pointed out in 1 and 2, above, writing for yourself will automatically have a higher level of quality without you even trying too hard.

***Writing for the market*** means that you have done the research, seen what's selling well right now, and are writing to that genre not because you like it specifically (though you may, and you may still simply enjoy writing), but mostly because you want to write a book with a built-in strong market.

This is also a solid approach, with just as many benefits as writing for yourself. The downsides of this approach are that you are possibly going to be writing a genre or field that you are not a huge fan of, or not an expert in. More research is needed – whether that is simply reading a collection of the best-selling fiction of the genre, or actual research into the non-fiction topic you have chosen.

Speaking of which, you will rarely see this approach used for non-fiction. The research needed to write a strong-selling book in a field you don't already have a solid knowledge base in is simply too much. The books that sell well in a particular non-fiction field sell well not because someone did a bunch of research just for the book, but because they already have the knowledge: typically through years of education, experience, and a passion for it. So really, pursuing this path for non-fiction is typically not just done.

But for fiction, it can make your book a lot easier to sell. You've got a built-in market for it, after all. However, the process of really finding, choosing, and researching what genre of fiction is currently selling well can prove difficult in your circumstance. You'll need to do a lot of research online to find out what genres are selling well right now, and then you'll need to order some of those books that are selling well (and possibly some that aren't). Reading them will help you understand what it is that makes them sell well. You may also want to do even more research, such as Facebook groups or other forums where fans discuss their favorite books. And then, finally, start writing your own. And it's possible you just don't have the background or the knack for that particular genre.

For that reason, I can't say that I really recommend writing for market in your current situation. Again, if you have the means, desire, and drive to do so – it's a great option. It just becomes a little harder when you don't have easy access to the resources you need. But if you do have access to the web, here are a couple of good places to start when looking for what genres are selling well:

Amazon.com (just look at sales numbers for the different genres to get a feel for them)

Authorearnings.com

thecreativepenn.com/genre

## Chapter 6

## Read More Books

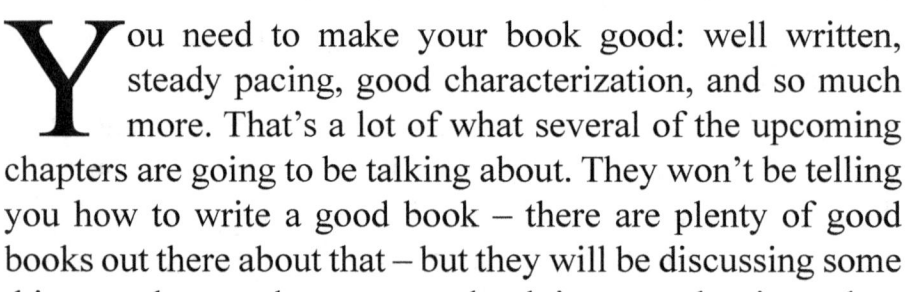

Y ou need to make your book good: well written, steady pacing, good characterization, and so much more. That's a lot of what several of the upcoming chapters are going to be talking about. They won't be telling you how to write a good book – there are plenty of good books out there about that – but they will be discussing some things to do to make sure your book is as good as it can be.

But you should also be able to simply know, overall, from immersion, what makes a good book. What do I mean by immersion? I mean you need to read a lot of books. *Immerse* yourself in them. Read books that are in the genre that you yourself are writing/have written. See what other people are putting out there. What drew you into those books? What made you back up and shake your head in disagreement?

Just… learn from them. Read them, enjoy them. Read some more. Every book you read makes you a better writer.

It is often said that there are two things a writer needs to do: Read, and Write. You need to do a lot of both. Writing more is obvious – the more you write, the better your craft becomes through practice, revision, etc. But reading will do the same for you. You will get a better understanding of good sentence flow. You'll expand your vocabulary. You'll see better how to use words you already know, or think you know. You'll understand your chosen field of writing better. There are so many reasons to just *read more*. And frankly, it's a great way to pass the time. For many of us, it's what drew us into writing in the first place – our love of books. Indulge in that love and do so with no regret knowing that 'hey, I'm *working!*'

## Chapter 7

## Read Even More Books

Okay, specifically, you need to read more books on *The Craft*. Read books on how to write. There are a lot of them out there. One of the most famous is of course the one by Stephen King, *On Writing* – but of course it is, it's by Stephen King. There are a lot of others out there as well. I can give you a list of my favorites, but this is very subjective. Take a look at some that look good to you – or have your people on the outside choose some. I'll include a list of some good options in the appendices, in case your people don't have time to track some down for you.

Also, read more books on marketing. Yes, this book is amazing. It's frankly one of the best out there on the subject of marketing. How do I know this? I wrote the book. That means I'm an expert on it. And as an expert on this book,

I can say with authority that it is the best book of its kind. (Yes, this is very circular logic – and biased, as well. I promise I'm done praising myself – at least for a couple pages).

There are plenty of good books on marketing out there. This one was written with a very specific set of circumstances in mind – but everyone is different, even within the prison system. Some of you may have a lot of money to dump into advertising. Some of you may have people with a lot of time and the willingness to do a lot of footwork for you. Some of you will have circumstances that I can't even imagine, with advantages and disadvantages peculiar to your situation. So please pick up and read a few more marketing books – there may be ideas in there that would work very well for you, but which I didn't include because either I don't like them myself, or because I felt that they wouldn't apply to most of the people this book is targeted towards.

Also, perhaps you're getting out soon. Many of those books will have some great ideas on how to further your goals; ideas that you will be able to start working on once you're outside the walls! And trust me, the time you have for reading will be severely cut down short once you get out. Take advantage of the time you have now.

# Part II

# Before You Publish...

CHAPTER 8

REVISE!

You've written a great book, have you? Well, you can make it better. Yes, you. Not an editor or your buddy down the hall; you. The first thing you need to do, though, is set it aside and let it age for a bit. Not long; a week, maybe a month. It depends on you. You will find that, unlike a fine wine, it will not age well. After some time apart from your creation you will begin to see its flaws, its warts, its blemishes. But now that you can see them even more clearly... you can fix them.

And fix them you must! Do not be afraid to strike out what needs to be removed, change what needs to be reworded or altered entirely, and add in scenes that need to be there but weren't.

The key to this is setting it aside. If you go through it right after you've completed it, the book is still too fresh, your writing too familiar to your eye and your mind. But after a couple weeks, with some distance, you will see it with a fresher, different view. You will see its flaws better, and perhaps see what needs to be enhanced to make the good, great.

Don't fall into the trap so many fall into: you have to stop eventually. Some authors revise, revise, revise. They always see flaws with every read-through (sometimes even when there are none); and with this obsession, the book is never done. And you can't give readers the book they need – your book – if you never stop revising it and never publish it. Set a limit for yourself. Decide: two revisions, and that's it. Then, you can move on to some of the other steps we will get into momentarily. But *do* revise, and then *stop* revising.

## Chapter 9

## Beta Readers!

Once you've done your revision (you did stop revising it, right?), it's time to let others read it. This will be more difficult than you might think for a couple reasons. One (which may not apply to you) is that you are actively looking for criticism, and that can be hard to receive when it's about something that you have worked so long on.

The other reason it may be difficult is that it can be hard to find people who will be honest with you. People you know won't want to hurt your feelings, or make you feel bad. They know how hard you've worked on your book, and how much time it has taken. Not only that, they may also come into it with a bias: "My good buddy wrote this, and I know he's a good writer. This is going to be good!" This makes them see it all in a more positive light than they should go into it with.

For this second reason, it can often be best to find beta readers who do not even know you personally. But perhaps I get ahead of myself. What even *is* a beta reader?

A beta reader is someone who reads your book before any of the public does, and lets you know how well it's working. Ideally, it will be someone who reads a lot, and understands what they should be looking for that makes a book a quality read. In addition, you should provide them with a list of questions that you could use to improve the book. These could be anything, but for a few examples:

> Was Chapter 4 in the right place, or would that scene do better later in the book?
> Did you feel a connection with Keenan?
> What did you think of the relationship between John and Alice?
> Did you understand why Kevin felt he had to do what he did?
> Did Chapter 8 flow well?

Ask yourself: anything that you may be curious about, anything you may be uncertain about, anything that you feel is important to the story – you should question it.

Where can you get a good beta reader? Well, normally I'd give any number of websites where professional beta readers can be found – or even well qualified amateurs. And certainly, you can have your people on the outside look into such things. There are many reader groups on facebook, and another good site is https://www.goodreads.com/group/show/50920-beta-reader-group. But for you, you have a large potential audience within the very walls in which you dwell. As mentioned earlier, you can ask your friends, people you know; but if you can find people who are not actively friends, that would be even better. Perhaps some of the people you know can pass it on to someone else that they know. Someone who won't have a problem telling you the parts of your book that should be improved. Who will tell you, honestly, what sucks and what doesn't.

If this isn't an option, or you simply can't find anyone who fits that mold, then ask your friends or family – but remind them that this process is very important to you as well, and not to spare your feelings. Let them know that their help will lead you to becoming as successful as possible.

Once you've gotten their feedback, make use of it. Your beta readers will likely pick out things you hadn't seen yourself. Fix what needs to be fixed. But remember, this is still YOUR story. And beta readers are not infallible. They are just opinions. You are free to ignore any or all of them. But especially consider any suggestion that more than one reader has made: if multiple of your beta readers say something is wrong, it's likely that your future readers may think so as well.

## Chapter 10

## Professional Edit

Once you've completed your revisions and made any changes you feel should be made based on the beta readers' input, it's time to have the professionals take a look at it.

Unfortunately, this is where we come to things you can't generally do within your institution. It's time to get an editor. Perhaps you have a professional editor in your midst – all kinds of people get locked up, after all; this isn't impossible. But more likely, you do not, or you are simply unaware of them. Which means this is the first time (but not the last) where I'm going to suggest you part with some of your hard-earned cash.

I know money can be very dear inside those walls; most prison jobs pay just pennies an hour (if you're even fortunate enough to be somewhere you have a job AND get paid for it). But if you have the means – whether it's from your accounts or assistance from family and friends – I strongly recommend a professional editor. It doesn't matter what sort of book you've written: urban novel or professional text; your book should be as free of grammatical, punctuation, spelling, or any other errors as you can make it. Yes, the story may be great; the lessons you impart and the information you convey could be important and well written; but when people start seeing errors of any sort, they get distracted. Those errors, especially if they are numerous, will begin to weigh on their mind and they can begin to lose respect for the book. *If there are this many errors the author didn't see or catch, is the actual information/story any good, either?* I know it seems silly, but human nature doesn't always make sense.

A professional editor can be very expensive. Even the cheap ones are expensive. I've heard it so often, "I simply can't afford an editor." And I understand – I'm not going to tell you to kill your dreams because you can't afford an editor. Get your book published, even if there may be typos you missed. In truth, I've found errors in books written by the best authors out there, books that have graced all the best-seller lists. So it won't *kill* your book, necessarily. But it *can* hurt it. And we are going for maximum readership and maximum profits, right? So, if you can afford it, get an editor. If you can't… well, go over your final text for mistakes as much as you can. Find the smartest guy in your institution and get him some commissary/store to check it over for you. Whatever you can do. In fact, let's see how good you do: there are errors I have left hidden in this very book. Let's see if you can find them! Let me know if you think you've spotted any typos or missed edits. There's no prize, but I love hearing from my readers for any reason, so this is a great excuse for that.

If you do have the funds, where can you get an editor? If you have people to go online for you, there are a lot of freelance editors out there. There is truly no shortage of editors out there willing to handle your project. One Facebook group that I've seen some good options in is simply titled "Services for Book Authors." Besides editors, you will find cover designers, layout people, marketing professionals, and much more.

Another site where your people can find a number of editors to choose from is https://aceseditors.org/resources/for-hire. I can't simply recommend any one editor for a number of reasons. One reason is that if I only mention one editor and all of you readers try to use that one editor, the editor would be overworked and no good to many of you. The other reason is that editors often have a specific genre (or a few specific genres) that they work with. So an editor who takes fiction might not handle any non-fiction. And even more, they might only handle specific types of fiction.

Again, if you need to (or want to) handle this yourself without your people having to be a constant intermediary, Cadmus Publishing does have a fantastic team of editors. They can assign one to you that fits your genre – and they will work directly with you. If there are other groups out there that reliably have this service for incarcerated authors, I don't know about them (but please let me know if you know of any – I'll be sure to put it up on my website so your people can get the information to you).

But Cadmus editors are certainly not the only ones out there. While Cadmus keeps their prices competitive, it is quite possible that your people can find a cheaper one that works well in your genre. If your people can find one that is cheaper and if they are able to reach out to them directly on your behalf, then that is money that could be going to marketing or other needs, so it could be well worth it.

## Chapter 11

## Cover!

"Never judge a book by its cover."

Yeah. I call BS on that one. Sure, it's good advice. For example, if you saw me in person, you'd never guess I knew 5 different forms of martial arts. And you'd be correct; I don't know any martial arts. So, good guess. But I *could* know all that... and still look the same.

But the fact is that, especially when it comes to the literal sense of that expression, people *do* judge books by their covers. Even I do. Every time. So if you want people to pick up your book once they've found it, you better dress to impress. Get that cover looking sharp. This is another one of those times where I am going to strongly recommend you break open your piggy bank and spend some of that money.

Look, even if you can draw really well, that doesn't mean you know what makes a cover "POP." It's not just about good artwork. It's layout; it's the font of the title; the size of the title; how the title is arranged; where the art itself draws the eye to; and so much more. Maybe you don't even need an actual image for your book. Especially with non-fiction books, sometimes it's just laying out the words in an appealing manner, or having some abstract design enhancing the look.

There are reasons professional artists typically attend art schools – there are specific ways to do this sort of thing that appeals to the eye. And if you want to sell your book, it needs to appeal to the eye.

So, hire a cover designer. There are lots to choose from. A great source of inexpensive designers is Fiverr.com. Also, the Facebook group "Services for Book Authors" typically has a good batch of cover designers hanging around. If you don't have people to hunt for these things for you, Cadmus Publishing does take inmate calls and have a wide array of cover artists on staff.

If you don't have the funds for a cover designer, at least get someone you trust to set it up for you. I've seen a lot of artwork that comes out of the prison, and frankly, there are a lot of artists in there I'd trust to do the artwork for any of my covers. In many cases they may also have a good eye for design and layout, so can help with the text (title, author name, etc) as well.

Finally, take a look at the covers of other books in your genre. Find the ones that really call out to you to read them. Then, consider what makes you like them. Apply them to your book. Show your artist what you see in them. Don't copy them, but consider what it is about them that talks to you. You don't have to reinvent the wheel, and you don't need to copy what others have done exactly. Instead, be inspired by them.

CHAPTER 12

# TITLE!

"Never judge a book by its... title."

Okay, that phrase doesn't exist. It was a cheap and easy reference to the last chapter. It made me chuckle in my head, so I put it here. But if the phrase *did* exist... it would be just as inaccurate as the original quote.

Your book's title is important. Along with the cover it is the first thing people will see. It should inform and engage. What do I mean by that? To begin with, it should inform. It should give at least some hint as to what lies inside. This can be very easy with a non-fiction book. Take this book, for example. The title pretty much tells you exactly what to expect within the covers. But even with fiction, your title should have at least *something* to do with the story within.

As to the 'engage' part? Simply put, you want the title to grab the reader. Something they read and think to themselves, "Hmmm… I wonder what that title is indicating?" The cover art and title of your book should pull your potential reader by the shoulders into the first room of your mind. Sometimes this can be something simple, one word. Sometimes you need a title *and* a subtitle – even a full dozen words! But whatever it is, choose it carefully. Think about it. Don't automatically take the first thing that pops into your head.

In fact, you should really shop your ideas around. What do I mean by this? Write down several options for your title and share them with friends and family. Ask them for their thoughts. What sounds the best to them? What makes them want to hear more? What flows best? Just get some input from people other than yourself, and make sure you looked at multiple options.

Finally, get inspiration from what's already out there – especially best-sellers. Look at your own bookshelf, or the shelf in the library. Find books that are relevant to what you wrote and consider the titles those authors used. Use them as a starting point for your own ideas. Don't copy them word-for-word, obviously – but you can still use them as a great jumping-off point.

## Chapter 13

## Layout

Open a book. Doesn't matter what book, though something in your genre would be ideal. Seriously – do this now; I'll wait. Open it up and take a look inside. Does it look good? Do your eyes float down the page easily or do they get caught up in distracting little issues? Does it have an easily readable font? Does it have a uniform look throughout?

These little issues are just the tip of the iceberg when it comes to laying out your book professionally. There are any number of items that go into a good layout, and I won't go into them in depth here; suffice to say, a good layout is important. When people take your book off the shelf and flip through it, deciding if they want to buy it, what are they going to see? A cobbled-together mess like the crazy ex you were lucky to get rid of? Or a flowing piece of textual art, one that invites the eye to smoothly follow down the page?

Look, we're still on the first impressions part of things. If people don't like the way a book looks, they are likely to not purchase it. Even if they get the book through Amazon or another online retailer, they typically have an option to 'look inside', where they can see how well put together the layout is.

Of the things I've covered so far – editing, beta readers, covers, etc – this one is probably the easiest to get away with if you need to do it yourself. Unfortunately, this is probably the one where you really *can't* do it yourself, because laying out a book is done exclusively on computers these days. You don't even need special software in many cases – MS Word can do the job in a pinch – but wherever you are publishing through will need digital files. So, whether you have your people publishing for you or you have a service you are doing it through, the layout will be set up digitally.

So make sure they are professionals (any professional service *should* be able to do at least a passable job) or make sure your people that are doing it are familiar with how books should look. Really, just at least make it *look* like a professionally done book. Again, if you're not sure what you should be doing, take a few books off your shelf and compare how yours is looking to how theirs looks. There should be some parallels, and your eyes and mind should not struggle to get through the pages.

## Chapter 14

## Pricing!

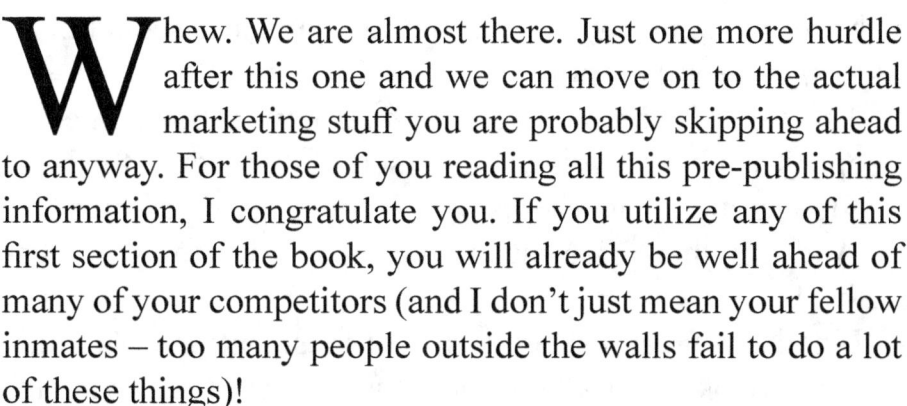

Whew. We are almost there. Just one more hurdle after this one and we can move on to the actual marketing stuff you are probably skipping ahead to anyway. For those of you reading all this pre-publishing information, I congratulate you. If you utilize any of this first section of the book, you will already be well ahead of many of your competitors (and I don't just mean your fellow inmates – too many people outside the walls fail to do a lot of these things)!

For now, let's talk money. *Oh yeah!* Specifically, how much are you going to charge for your book? This is an important question with a few good answers.

The first option is to price it as low as you can. The thinking behind this is that if you can get more people to buy the book, then you are making more sales that yield more royalties! Not only that, every additional person that buys your book is possibly talking to their friends and family about it... and *those* friends and family may also go on to buy the book and perhaps tell their friends and family about it, and on and on!

This is a solid strategy, for the reasons already outlined above.

Another option is to price it higher than the minimum. There is a thing called "Perceived Value" in marketing and sales. The idea is that, if a person sees a higher price tag on one thing than on another similar item, they often assume that there is a reason for that higher price. Whether it's higher quality, more 'stuff', even just a better return policy – they feel that the higher priced item is the better one, and will purchase that one, despite the higher price. You see this in almost all industries – people assume the higher-priced item is better in some way, even if the two things are equal in all aspects except the price.

The same 'Perceived Value' *can* apply to book sales. If people see a higher price, they assume it's because the book is good enough that other people are willing to pay more for it. And a higher price means more royalties for you, dear author!

Finally, you can use a mixture of these options. You may start the book off at a low price; then, when it really begins selling, bring that price up to make more on each copy sold! This only works if you do manage to get some significant sales, and ideally some great reviews. But it is certainly something to keep in mind.

There will be restrictions on how low you can price the book, obviously. Be sure that whatever you price it at, you are making SOMETHING, or at least breaking even. Keep in mind that there are costs that go into the sale of each book. There is obviously the cost of printing the book itself. But also, any retailer that sells your book will be taking a percentage of the sale as well. This is typically going to be around half the price of the book! If you publish directly through Amazon, you won't be paying them as much from each sale and therefore get to keep a greater percentage of the profits. But you will only be able to sell the book through them, and likely will have even more difficulty in getting it into other stores, libraries, etc.

Chapter 15

Metadata

Okay, what the hell is metadata?
To put it simply, metadata is the information *about* your book. What genre is it? What are its BISAC codes (pretty much the same thing as genre)? What keywords are associated with it? Even things like the synopsis and the author bio can be part of the metadata.

And these things are very important. When someone is looking for a werewolf story, if you don't have the word werewolf in your title or keywords, even if you have werewolves throughout the book, they won't see your book come up *at all* on their search. You can have several keywords with most sellers (i.e., Amazon, Barnes & Noble, etc) – and I recommend using as many of them as you can; each keyword means that your book can pop up when a reader is looking for it.

Remember that although the term is *'keyword'*, it doesn't have to be just one word. Let me give you an obvious, simple example. 'Marketing' is a keyword, but that's pretty vague – marketing can apply to all kinds of topics, not just book marketing. One of the keywords that will be used for this book is 'book marketing'. Two words, but still considered one keyword.

BISAC codes are not just important, they are actually necessary. (BISAC = Book Industry Standards And Communications, in case you were wondering. I know, that doesn't really tell you much more than the acronym. Gimme a second.) This is how the online and physical booksellers will organize your book. This tells them which established genre your book fits into. With keywords, you can use any word you want. For a BISAC, though, they are well established and you will need to choose from the options available. You can find the full list at https://bisg.org/page/BISACEdition. I'd print them here, but there are a ton of them. Literally thousands.

Your BISAC code could be pretty generic: 'fiction, general' is a code (FIC000000, if you're curious). But you will find yourself getting better results if you get as specific as possible. FIC042120 is 'Fiction/Christian/Romance/Suspense. Pretty specific. But this code could work well for a book about a nun who leaves the convent to work for the government as an international spy, wooing men along the way with her seeming innocence. (Hmmm… mental note for new book series…).

The nice thing about FIC042120 is that if someone is just looking for a Christian book, this will show up. If someone is looking for a Romance, this book will show up. If someone is looking for a fiction romance, this will show up. Any grouping of those genres will reveal your new title, *Nun Too Good, Book III: Chasing the Devil of Prague*. And most sites will take up to three BISAC codes, so you still have two more you can put in!

One can argue that BISAC codes are more powerful, but keywords are more flexible. Use both to your advantage.

Next on the metadata list we have the synopsis. ***I CANNOT OVEREMPHASIZE HOW IMPORTANT THIS IS!*** You can tell it's important because it's in caps, bold, *and* italics. Along with the cover, this will be what leads people to buy the book or ignore it (once they've found it, of course). This is your sales pitch. This is what you need to use to hook the reader. This should be your best piece of writing you put forth. Tell the reader what awaits them in your pages. Entice them. Make them want more. However, like writing the book itself, this is an art, not a science. Much of what will make this good can only come from you. But there are a few items to consider, a few tricks of the trade.

Read the descriptions for other books in your genre. See what works on you. What grabs you? If it is a book you've read, what was it about the description that made you want to read it? What got you excited about it? What sort of language did they use? Don't plagiarize their description, obviously, but consider the actual words they use, and if some of them are powerful terms you may want to use them in your own synopsis.

For fiction novels the first sentence or two should be the real hook. Maybe just eight or ten words that give a powerful impact. Then, go into more detail about the overall plot, explaining some of what those first words are hinting at. And don't be afraid of hyperbole. Using words that seem often overused, like 'once-in-a-lifetime adventure', or 'stunning', 'extreme' – while clichés should be generally avoided in your writing, they can be used (in moderation and appropriately) in a synopsis.

For non-fiction, consider what you are instructing the reader in; what problem, issue, or obstacle are you helping them to overcome? What are you teaching them? Don't get overly technical, using terms from the book that the reader may or might not understand. In the description for *this* book, you will not see terms like 'metadata', 'BISAC', or even 'writing for yourself'. For this book, the synopsis will discuss the problem I'm helping you with: marketing your book. It may be something along the lines of, "Prison can't stop you from successfully marketing your book, and I'm here to tell you what steps you can take from where you are!"

You can even hire a professional copywriter to write it for you – though I generally don't recommend it. Nobody knows your book as well as you do. It can also be expensive; after all, the person who writes the sales blurb/synopsis has to know your book, so they will be spending a few hours reading or at least skimming through it so they know what to say about it.

Your author bio is the last thing we'll discuss here. I'd say it is the least important of what we've discussed in this chapter, but that doesn't mean you can just dismiss it. Your author bio is where you will let people know about you – and that will tell them a little about what to expect in your book. Most importantly, an author bio gives people a little bit of a sense that they know you, personally. This little bit allows you to connect with your reader on a more personal level.

One question that comes up here – in your situation of being incarcerated – is how much of yourself should you tell? When I've worked with incarcerated authors, a common question is if they should use a pseudonym. This really depends on a number of factors, primarily 1) What genre is the book; and 2) What was your crime?

If you're writing an urban book, or a book about prison, or anything where your criminal history can actually lend credibility to what you are writing, then you should seriously consider using your real name (or your street name, but with your real name not being hidden deliberately). If you are writing a book of the sort where having a criminal background could interfere with your credibility, then you may wish to use a pseudonym. A good example of this is any non-fiction book that does not have anything to do with your criminal history. This is not a hard-and-fast rule, however. For example, if you are writing a book about investing and you were convicted of investment fraud of any sort, you should really consider your options for a pseudonym. On the one hand: your background in finance is probably easily verified; you may have an abundance of knowledge of finance – you just got convicted because you were trying to take shortcuts. But you do know the best ways to legally do things. So you are good at it, and people can see that when they look at your history. This lends credence to your authority as a finance writer.

On the other hand, people may have difficulty seeing past your criminal history with fraud and be concerned that the strategies, tips, etc that you espouse in your book may not be fully ethical or perhaps may even be illegal. This is a hurdle you would need to overcome.

In a similar vein, your criminal background may matter for other books, too. If you are convicted of any violent crime, for example, but have written a really good children's book, your reputation may tarnish how people view your cute book about the worm who couldn't make it home for supper. And with the internet, people can search your author name far too easily.

If you do use a pseudonym for these reasons, be sure you use it consistently. For example, if you register your copyright with the government, you can register the book using your pseudonym. You will use your real name on the application as well, but your pseudonym will be the name visible to the public.

# Part III

# Actual Marketing Stuff

CHAPTER 16

## INTRODUCTION: REPRISE

Okay – here's where we get to the real meat of marketing a book. The stuff that you're going to do to put your work under everyone's eyes.

But let me warn you – if you skipped Part II, you are doing yourself a strong disservice. While the tips, suggestions, and ideas in Part II may not be the type of thing you think of when you think of 'marketing' – trust me, they are just as important as having a good ad placed on the right platform or whatever else you may do to get your book sold. Of course, if your book is already written and published, it's a bit late to go back and take many of those suggestions. But if you really want to succeed, you are going to write more books, not just this one (I'll talk about why in a chapter dedicated to writing multiple books, later on). And you will want to have that information for your next projects. So don't forget to go back and read Part II.

But, yes, this is where we really start in on the meat of what people consider marketing. As I mentioned earlier, oh so long ago, "50% of marketing is successful – we just don't know which 50%." So, there's a lot of options in this book for you (and a lot more that I won't cover due to them being near impossible to do from in prison) – but there is no way to tell which ones will work for you and your book. Your own judgement will be coming in to play. It will be up to you to decide which parts of this book to utilize and which you cannot or choose not to do. My advice, though, to start with – do as much of it as you can, and do it a lot. There's no such thing as *'too much marketing'*. It simply doesn't exist.

However, you can easily blow a budget on marketing; and if it's not the right kind for you, you may not sell enough books to recover what you spent. So judge for yourself which options are right for you. I'll do my best to give you as much info, pro and con, about the options available to you – but it's your call in the end.

But the free stuff? The stuff that just takes time? Do as much of that stuff as you can! And that's what the next few chapters are all about.

Chapter 17

# Letter Writing

Look, this is one of the most obvious options available to you. While not technically free, it's pretty darn close. For the cost of a stamp and some paper, you can reach out to people who can make your book known to dozens, hundreds, thousands, or even millions of people.

However, the higher up that number scale you go (dozens/hundreds/thousands/millions), the less likely that that person will do anything for you. Hell, it's quite possible they won't even *see* your letter themselves. You want to send a letter to Oprah? Sure, go ahead. It doesn't cost much. But that letter will be competing with thousands of others (for just one day's worth of mail!) and go through a gauntlet of a dozen people who have to decide if it's worth kicking up to

Oprah herself, or someone qualified to say 'yes' in her name. The odds, my friend, are not in your favor.

But send a letter to someone who can only influence a dozen people (like their friends and families) and it's pretty much guaranteed they'll see it themselves. What they choose to do with it is of course up to them.

Of course, you may be in a rarefied position. As a convicted felon it is possible that your history has made you of interest to someone in a higher position. This is another one of those times where you have an advantage over the typical Joe Schmoe out here in the free world. Depending on your criminal background, people may be even more curious about seeing what you have to say and may be *more* likely to open a letter from you and (if relevant) pass it up to the person of influence you were trying to reach. I'm not saying Oprah is going to read your letter herself… but the truth is, depending on the crime you were convicted of you quite possibly have a better chance of getting her attention than I ever will, for example. (Hey – if you do get her attention, tell her I have a project she might be interested in, about a spy who's also a nun…)

So, dream big. It only costs a stamp. Just realize that it is quite likely those letters won't reach their intended audience.

But, who else should you write to? And what should you say?

The list of who you should write to is essentially endless. Start out by reaching out to anyone you've known who might be interested in the very fact that you wrote and published a book. Even if they are not interested in the subject matter of the book, the fact that you are a published author is enough for most people to at least take note of. Publishing a book immediately lends you a certain amount of status – it's not something just anyone has done. So, many people you know may well buy the book – or tell their friends/family/co-workers about it – just because they now know someone who wrote a book.

Beyond that, reach out to all your old mentors and authority figures. Your teachers will be very pleased to hear all their effort didn't go to waste and will almost always be truly interested in what it is you have created. Many – especially your language/English teachers, will see it as a personal victory that they have contributed to. I'm not saying any or all of them will buy your book – keep that fact (that not everyone you contact will buy your book) in mind for every group we discuss here – but they don't need to. The key thing in all marketing and publicity is simply to *get the word out*. And some will buy it. And some will talk about it. Which will lead to others buying it. So reach out to your teachers, your principals, your babysitter, the guy who runs the candy store you used to hang out in all the time; hell, drop a note to your judge, or even your prosecutor.

Find the addresses of your hometown's libraries and small 'mom-and-pop' bookstores. Let them know about your book. For these types of places be sure to let them know the ISBN number, in case they decide to order some for their shelves. A lot of bookstores have a special section reserved specifically for books by 'local authors'. And how local do you have to be? City, county, sometimes even the state can be considered 'local'. Give it a try. And don't forget your school's library (assuming your book is appropriate for a school).

Do you have a talk show you listen to on the radio? Send a letter to them. Local news? Now, you can send a letter, but for more news-oriented outlets, you might want to consider a press release; we will dive deeper into that in a later chapter. I'm not saying that a press release is the better option – in many cases it is not – but do consider and weigh the choices. Personally, I have found that a letter will trump a press release just about every time, if it is written well, contains the right content, and is directed to the right person. But a press release is still something to consider.

Think hard about what you say in your letter. First, don't make it *look* like a form letter. It's fine if you want to use basically the same letter for several people, but don't make it obvious. Your letters should each look like they were written specifically for the person you are sending it to. Sometimes, it helps to have just a couple lines at the beginning that talk to the person individually, and then the rest can be copied from another letter. Because everyone likes to think that you composed the letter for them personally, and thought of them specifically for this letter.

What should the letter include? Well, the obvious information like the fact that you wrote a book, what it's about, etc. But it should also talk about why they should give a rip about it, or you for that matter. Appeal to them as a human being, not as a person who will help you sell your book. A good start for inmates is to tell the person about how the journey to becoming an author has improved you. Perhaps, how you feel that this is finally something you can contribute to society, even from the circumstances you find yourself in, now. The simple fact is that when people first receive your letter they probably aren't going to care about your book.

They have no evidence that it's any good, or that you can tell a compelling story (fiction or non-fiction). So you have to impress them with that letter, and give them a reason to care about you and your project. Finally, you have to show them that their support of your project isn't going to be something they regret. I'm not talking about cash or how they can profit from supporting you. Many of the people you will write to are already doing well enough, and will be frankly skeptical that they could gain anything monetarily from your project. What you want to show them is that by supporting you and your book, they are making a positive difference in the world, or even just their community.

Also, don't forget to mention in your letter what you want. Straight up say it (though do it politely, perhaps even meekly). "It would mean a lot to me if you could take the time to read my book. I've worked very hard on it, and I feel that I am finally able to do something positive and contribute to society in a way that will outlast me in a manner I can feel proud of. If you find the book worthy, I would be honored if you could tell your audience about it."

Take your time on the letters. Revise them. Share them with others for feedback. Like writing a book, writing a letter is an art. *Perfect them before you send them.* This is actually very important. If your letter reads like it was written by a ten year old... how is the recipient going to believe that your book is any better? Re-read, revise, correct. Make that letter a paragon of literature, itself. Write a letter that you could turn in to an English teacher knowing that you just got an 'A' on it.

I don't think I can emphasize enough how much good this simple task of writing letters can do for you. Some of the most successful authors I know got that way through dedicated letter-writing. Interviews, magazine articles, even actual financial assistance for marketing their book or getting their next book published – all because they wrote letters. The most successful ones sent out a *lot* of letters: dozens each day, in some cases. But keep writing them and good things are bound to come of it.

CHAPTER 18

WORD OF MOUTH

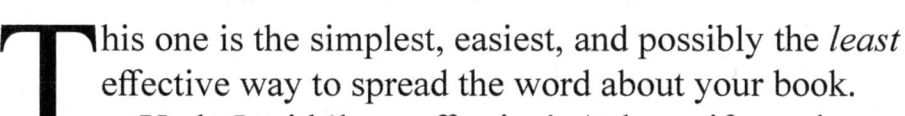

This one is the simplest, easiest, and possibly the *least* effective way to spread the word about your book.

Yeah, I said 'least effective'. At least, if you do everything else right. The fact is, you can only reach so many people by word of mouth. The theory is that those people will tell others, who will tell others, who will also tell others... and on and on. And in that sense, everything we do will rely on word of mouth. Even the letter-writing we discussed last chapter has a large element of 'word of mouth'. And in that sense, word of mouth will become very important to your campaign and will have a strong effect.

But what I'm trying to tell you is that you cannot rely on this by itself. You only know so many people. And let's say you tell 100 people... they are not all going to tell everyone they know. And when they do, those people will forget about it in the most important sense. They won't buy a copy right then, and they won't do it later. They'll still know that you wrote a book, and it may come up sometime when they're talking to their friends about a guy they know (or just know *of*) who wrote a book from prison. But this is not something you can rely on. Remember I mentioned earlier that repetition is very important in any marketing campaign, and word of mouth just doesn't do that. Not by itself. Letter writing does better than straight word of mouth partly because you have a longer reach with a letter than with your voice (even with a phone), but with a letter it is written down. And when they see that letter on their desk in five minutes, they'll think about it again. And when they move it somewhere else, they'll think about it again. And if it's sent to a business (or a show, or newspaper, or whatever) they have something concrete in their hands they can refer to while deciding to do something about it.

So word of mouth is important – it will play into most other forms of marketing and publicity you utilize, in one way or another. But by itself, it is nothing.

## Chapter 19

## Submitting Articles

You're a writer, right? I mean, you wrote a book. So how about using that talent to further your publicity goals?

No media company relies exclusively on in-house writers for their articles. All of them – magazines, newspapers, websites – get at least some of their articles from 'contributors'. In other words, people who say, "Hey, I wrote this article on something that interests your readers. Want to publish/post it? And maybe even give me a few bucks?"

This could be you. In fact, it SHOULD be you. Whatever it is you wrote about, you are now qualified to write an article on a related topic. Did you write about prison reform? Submit something to PLN. Did you write about how you found God? Submit something to any of the dozens of religious magazines. Heck, even if only one chapter details how you found God (for example), and the rest of the book was about how you grew up on the streets, got into trouble, and found yourself arrested… as long as you've got that one chapter in there, you can use that as your credentials to write an article about it. Wrote a romance? There are a lot of magazines and websites about writing in general. Or perhaps a site or magazine about relationships. Did you write a fantasy epic? Maybe an article for *Dragon* magazine, or any of the smaller options or websites out there.

No matter what you wrote about, there is an article you could write, as well.

How to submit the article will vary with each outlet. Some are fine with you just sending the article in already written. Some like you to present a 'proposal' of the topic you want to write about. Most will ask about your writing credentials (especially if you're only submitting a proposal).

How will this help market your book? Well, first off, you may find a spot in the article itself to slide in a reference about your book. I don't generally recommend this; it can seem very self-serving. More commonly, at the end of the article will be a small blurb about who you are. Something along the lines of "Francis Raemond is a marketing professional in the Pacific Northwest, and has just released his latest book, *The Inmate's Guide to Success as an Author*."

If people like your writing style in the article, if they like what you had to say on the subject, if they want to read more about your ideas, now they can seek you out and find your book for more.

And even if they don't… many places will throw you a few dollars for the article itself.

What should you write about? Well, that's going to depend mostly on what you've already written about. Beyond that... look at what else is being written where you want to submit an article. Find something that you can lend a unique perspective on. Again, you have a bit of a unique advantage here: not many people can write – about any topic – from the perspective that you have due to your current situation. If at all possible, leverage that unique viewpoint in your article. Perhaps it can even be the focal point of the piece. Many people have written about COVID; and many have written about how it is affecting our prison system. But only a very few have written about how it affects the prison system or the inmates themselves from the perspective you have, as one of those inmates. You may not have much medical knowledge; you may not be an expert on the politics, or the financial ramifications the prisons faced during COVID, but by god, you know first-hand what happened behind the walls. You know things even the guards don't know about. Use your unique situation. As I've said before in this book and will say again – you have a unique opportunity due to your unpleasant circumstances; at least get something good out of it if you can. Make your incarceration work for you, instead of against you, for a change.

Finally, don't be discouraged by rejection. It's easier to get an article published than a book... but it's still not a walk in the park. Keep writing, keep submitting, keep trying. This can be an invaluable opportunity for free publicity, targeted to your specific reading population.

## Chapter 20

## Interviews

Interviews aren't possible for everyone; and even for those of you who can do this, you may not have the opportunity. But in the course of your letter-writing you can let the media know that you are available for interviews. Interviews can be HUGE publicity opportunities. Whether it's radio, television, magazine, or even for a podcast – an interview (on any subject) can be a huge boost to your sales and cost you nothing.

Magazine interviews are one of the best options. In many cases, this is done strictly in writing. They'll send you a list of questions by mail (or email), and you will respond in writing as well. They may publish the interview verbatim, but it will also typically be done along with a relevant article on whatever topic the interview was about. And when I say 'magazine' I really mean any type of written interview: magazine, internet, newspaper, etc.

Radio interviews can be a little more difficult to manage. This would obviously be done by phone, and can often be pre-recorded, not broadcast live. This allows the radio host to do some basic editing, which is very handy with the recorded interruptions on your end, as well as the (typically) fifteen-minute time limit most inmates have for each phone call. Such an interview can take place over multiple phone calls, and then get edited together for one interview. Some institutions simply do not allow interviews, so be aware of the rules for your joint.

Television interviews are very hard to get, but it does happen. Sometimes it happens for reasons other than what you might be wanting to talk about (your book), but they can still be valuable for promotion. Obviously, this needs to be set up and approved by your institution; typically the interviewer, not you, will be the one to handle this end of it.

In any of these cases, you may be interviewing on a topic that is NOT your book. That is fine. Just be sure to get a mention of your book in at some point and remind your interviewer (ideally before you start) that you'd like to promote the book, asking if they can mention it again after the interview. Most are happy to do so.

If possible, get a copy of the interview for your webpage or other promotional endeavors. If it's a radio, podcast, or television interview, ask them for the URL the interview can be found at online, and put the link to it on your webpage (or the actual audio/video, if that is an option).

Lastly, be aware that there are places that will be willing to do an interview but that charge a 'promotional fee' or some other such thing. Sometimes this can be as little as $50, but it can range into the thousands. If you are considering one of these options, be sure to find out some information first. Where does the interview appear? What is their typical viewership/readership/etc (in other words, how many people are likely to see/hear the interview)? What is their typical demographic (what sorts of people listen/view/etc)? These can be useful to know even if you aren't paying for the interview but become vital when deciding if your money will be well spent when paying for one. Obviously, you want to seek out the normal, free interviews, but sometimes the paid option is not bad, either.

## Chapter 21

# Brick & Mortar

It's pretty much every author's dream to walk into Barnes & Noble and see their book on the shelves. Maybe even in a display at the front of the store. This is not an impossible dream, but let's start a little closer to home, a little smaller.

Getting your book into B&N is a difficult task, at best. Even if you lived right next door to one, even if you were the manager of one, you probably couldn't get your book on the shelf at your local Barnes & Noble. The reason for this is corporate structure and policy. Individual B&N stores are told by the corporate head honchos what books go on their shelves. They really don't have much, if any, latitude for making their own choices locally.

So, let's shelve that idea for a moment. (See what I did there? Shelve the idea? Like, you know, a bookstore shelf? … I don't know why I bother.) Anyway, let's focus on the smaller bookstores, where the people who work there can have some say on what goes on the shelf. You will probably be able to speak to the owner, as well.

This is a common start to getting your book into physical stores. Find your local bookstores and reach out to them. Often, they have a special section in their store dedicated exclusively to local authors. What is local? Well, I'm not referring to where you may currently be residing, obviously. I mean the place you grew up, or the place where you were living your adult life. Either one can count you as a 'local'. Bonus points if you actually name the town or the area in your author bio on the back or inside back cover!

How do you approach the bookstore with your book, though? Well, just do it. You have a few options. Personal appearances are the best option. Have your family bring a copy of the book to the shop and ask to speak with whoever makes the ordering decisions. Let that person know what the book is about and your personal connection to the area (grew up there, moved there as an adult, went to school in the area, etc). Be sure that your book can be ordered through their regular channels. Most indie publishers should be able to handle this – but check with your publisher. If you self-published, check your distributor to ensure its availability to small shops. Ingram Spark is a great self-publishing company, and they have full access to all the usual channels, which means your book can be easily purchased by bookstores and libraries. Also be sure that you have allocated enough of your book's cover price to go to the retailer; 40-

55% is standard, though it's best if you go on the higher end of that. This means that if your book's cover price is $10, the bookstore would like to be able to keep $5 of that. I know it may seem like a lot, but this is the typical cut they get.

Besides bookstores, be sure to reach out to libraries, as well. Again, start with libraries that are or were local to you. There really isn't much difference in how you approach libraries versus how you approach book stores. In the library, you will still be asking for the head librarian or whoever makes the decision on which books to put on the shelves.

Be confident. You won't always get on the shelves… but it does not hurt to try.

Chapter 22

# Keep Copies Handy

It used to be that if you self-published a book through a small press you'd need to order a run of 1,000 books or more. Then, you'd have to store them in your garage and hope you could get rid of all of them. This was expensive to begin with, and authors would wind up having that first run of books sitting in their garage for years to follow. This was especially true since it was then – as it is now – almost impossible to get any nationwide bookstores to carry your book on the shelves. So how did these authors sell them? Not easily... but in many cases they were still able to get a good number of them sold.

With the age of Print on Demand (PoD), having a stockpile of 1,000 books simply isn't necessary anymore. Of course, Large Publishers (Random House, Penguin, you know – those guys) will print huge runs of tens of thousands of copies or more; but most smaller presses will simply use PoD. And this means that it is much easier and cheaper for you to publish your book, since you don't have to pay that initial cost to print a ton of copies of it and then store them somewhere while you try to sell them.

However, you should still keep a couple dozen copies on hand. Obviously your storage is limited, but if you are able, keep a few copies in your locker and see to it that your people on the outside have a bunch, as well.

Every now and then someone will show an interest in purchasing a copy of the book. Why not make it easy for them, save them some money on shipping, and get yourself a couple of extra bucks (because the reseller always takes their massive cut) and hand them over a copy right there for the right price? Whether it's someone in the same housing unit as you who's paying with some commissary, or someone your mother runs into at the grocery store – it can be a quick, easy way to get your book out there. Besides all this, even if a person expresses an interest in buying the book, that doesn't mean they'll remember to do so later on. Get that book to them now, while they're still thinking about it and have you right in front of them. That's Salesmanship 101, right there.

I'm not saying this is going to rocket you to the best-seller lists. In fact, you may want to keep in mind that copies you sell yourself will not count toward any "Best-Seller" algorithm. But every little bit helps, you know? And you never know who you'll wind up handing that copy over to (and if you really want, you can simply give it away to the right people – friends, family, or people you meet that have some influence!).

## Chapter 23

## Magazine/Newspaper Ads

Print ads are one of the best forms of marketing available. They are also one of the most expensive. And often, the most poorly utilized.

When considering a print ad, understand that you are taking whatever money you are spending on the ad, and simply rolling the dice. It's a gamble. Whether it pays off or not, that money is spent. The simple fact is most authors don't use any print advertising. There are very good reasons for this but this is also something in your favor: the competition is thin.

Obviously, one of the big reasons that many authors eschew print ads is that they are simply expensive. They are also slow to print and get under the eyes of your potential readers, unlike internet ads that can appear instantly. In addition, you are paying for the ad even if literally no one so much as glances at it. Finally, print media doesn't have the circulation and power it once did. With the advent of the internet, people consume most of their periodicals online; whether it's magazines, newspapers, etc. Obviously, this isn't completely the case. Print is not dead, people still read physical newspapers, magazines, and the like, just not in the numbers they once did.

But it is still expensive to place an ad. As an (extreme) example, a half-page, black and white ad in ONE issue of Reader's Digest is over $43,000. USA Today? How about $31,000 for a 1/16th page ad. For one day.

Of course, these are large circulation, prestigious periodicals. But even your smaller city newspapers can run a few hundred for a single, small ad in one issue.

But sometimes, your target demographic will have a magazine that addresses them. Let's go with something familiar: Prison Legal News. A single ad, 1/6th of a page (their smallest size) will run you $190 for one issue. As with any other media, if you run it for more than one issue, it will cost less per issue (but more overall). So, if you think one of the groups of readers for your book will be inmates, this is a solid option.

And in most cases, there is a magazine dedicated to whatever sector you will be writing for. This is especially true for non-fiction books, but for fiction, as well. Writing science fiction or fantasy? How about *Asimov's*? Do you write mystery? *Ellery Queen* is the one for you. There are options for pretty much anything. And the more narrow the audience it caters to, the less the ad will cost. Keep in mind, though, the reason for this is that it will have a smaller readership; so fewer people will see the ad. But if they're already reading about your topic, there's a strong chance they will be interested in what you've written, too.

Finally, we come to the hard part of advertising in print: Getting the ad to the magazine/newspaper/whatever. They are going to require a digital file. You can't just draw something up on paper and send it in to them. You can't even create something on a computer, print it up, and send it in. For this part of it, you will almost certainly need outside help.

More importantly, you will probably need professional help. Anyone who sees your ad is going to judge your book based on how the ad looks. Even if you have a great cover, if the ad itself is poorly designed, they will disregard the entire thing (including the book itself) as amateurish and probably not good enough to spend their time or money on. So, be sure to find someone qualified to make a good ad.

## Chapter 24

## Online Advertising

Online advertising is huge. Like, seriously huge. You can potentially reach more eyeballs with this than with any print ad you might place. However, online advertising can be SO MUCH cheaper.

So, more eyes equals more sales, right? But cheaper usually means it's not as effective, right? *How can this dichotomy be?*

Well, it's just the way the interweb works. The thing is, more eyeballs seeing your ad does not mean that more people are buying it. It just means more people are seeing it. However, if done right, online advertising can totally beat out many different forms of print advertising. And how can it be cheaper? That's easy: CPC.

Yup. Just threw an acronym at you with no context. So, let me fill you in on the digital age of advertising. I will also say at this point that there is a lot to digital advertising I'm not going to go into. Other books cover it very well; if you have the resources to do this yourself or have your people dive deeper into it, I would recommend any of the books out there that focus on digital advertising. I'll just say that there is a lot you can do to optimize your results, but they can be very time consuming and research intensive.

So, back to CPC. CPC stands for *Cost Per Click*. What this means is that you don't pay for how many people *see* your ad, you pay for how many people *actually click* on it! That means that you're not paying for some schmuck who sees your ad, grunts in disinterest, and moves on. You are only paying for that beautiful person who sees your ad, thinks to themselves how interesting it looks, and actually *clicks on it* to find out more and possibly buy the book.

There are other pricing methods. Some are priced on *Impressions*, for example. Impressions is just how many people saw the ad. Avoid these.

There are a lot of places you can run your digital ad; a few examples are Google, Amazon, Facebook, etc. For this book we will only look at Facebook, since it is the easiest of the options for your people to do. After all, they are probably already on Facebook to begin with – and ideally, you should have a Facebook Author page (more on that in another chapter).

Allow me to give you a quick overview on the process. Once you set up the ad (again, I won't go into the details because interfaces change fairly frequently, especially small details like menu items, where to click, etc), you can set up a budget for how much you want to spend on it. Typically, it will be calculated as how much you want to spend per day, and how long you want the ad to run. So, if you want the ad to run for 3 months and have a budget of $300, then you would set it up to automatically end after three months (yes, it can do that for you – or run until you tell it to stop, if you prefer!), and that each month should have a budget of $100, or just over $3 per day.

I would suggest not going lower than $75 a month. Ideally, I would go higher than that. There is generally a point at which ads become significantly more impactful; there is no hard-and-fast rule for this, but I've found that anything under $75 does not yield any significant results.

You will also need to set up your target demographic. This simply means, what kind of people do you want to see your ad? From what countries, from what age groups, and with what sort of interests? For example, if your book is modern fantasy romance, you might want to target American (and/or other English speaking countries) females in the 16-50 age range, who have interests in keywords like: fantasy, magic, twilight, romance, witches, books, and reading. You should always include 'books, reading' and similar keywords and concepts – after all, if someone isn't interested in books or reading, they are not terribly likely to buy your book, are they?

Finally, where will you link the ad to? You could link it straight to the book's page on Amazon so they can read about it there and immediately purchase it. You could also link them to your personal author webpage if you have one (more on that in another chapter). Perhaps you prefer somewhere else, like Barnes & Noble. Ultimately, this choice is up to you. If you are advertising for just this one book, I would typically recommend linking to its Amazon page. If you have a series, you can still do this, but you might instead link them to your author webpage if you have a good one (they can still see it's part of a series from your Amazon page if it is set up right).

That's the simple stuff about Facebook ads. Obviously there is more to it than that, but your people on the outside will have to navigate the details themselves. There are many tutorials online about how to set up ads on Facebook that they can view.

As mentioned, there are other options out there: Google and Amazon are two big avenues that come to mind: Amazon because that's where most people go to buy books, and you can set your ad to appear when they are already buying or looking at another book in your genre; and Google because that's where people go for… well, everything. If they're looking for a good book on floral arrangements, they might simply google 'flower arrangement book' and see what comes up there.

Amazon and Google are a bit more complicated to set up and monitor, and since this is on someone else, I think it's less likely your people will be willing or able to do it. If they are, these are definitely options to consider – much of the information I give above about Facebook ads apply about equally to other online advertising.

## Chapter 25

## Press Release

Okay, so I know this section of the book is supposed to be stuff you can do yourself if you have the money... but really, most of it you will need at least a little outside help for.

Press releases are our first example of this. You can write up your own press release, and most of the work can be done by a PR distribution company. Frankly, any of them works pretty much as well as the other. PRNewsWire, Newswire, and Cision are probably the three largest, but there are many more out there as well.

Once you've written it, you have to get your press release *to* them so that they can distribute it. And this is done digitally, on the internet.

Overall, it's a pretty easy process, so I include it in this section of this book, rather than skipping it entirely. The hard work is writing out the press release. There are certain standard formulas that you'll want to consider, but keep in mind that you are basically writing a news article. Write it as though you were writing an article for a newspaper and that will be a good start. Once you have it well written, your people on the outside should be able to run through the process online to get it submitted and distributed pretty easily.

As a last resort you can send your press release out by snail mail, to media outlets you have tracked down information for. But I have to warn you that this will likely have almost no result. If this is your strategy, you will typically be better off just sending out interview requests or an offer to write an article for them (or the article itself).

Chapter 26

# Leveraging The Fact Of Your Incarceration; Also, Son Of Sam Laws

I've already mentioned this a few times throughout this book for specific circumstances, but keep in mind that some people will take an interest in what you have to say simply because you are incarcerated. The USA in particular has a strange obsession with crime and prisons. True crime shows are huge. There are even popular programs that show day-to-day life within the various prison systems.

Like everything else, the details and options will vary with your crime and with the topic of your book. But sometimes your situation can help you sell your product. If it's appropriate, don't be afraid to mention your past or your current circumstances in your press releases, your articles, and your letters to various luminaries or influencers.

In some cases, you may be compelled to discuss everything about your history while they basically ignore your book. This is fine. Get in what you can about the book, but remember that any publicity is good publicity in this case. If someone looks you up online, they will find the book and may be intrigued by what you have to say on your own, when given the chance.

This leads us to another question I've seen a lot: What about the 'Son of Sam' laws? It's not directly related to marketing, but I see it so often I thought I'd make a brief mention of it.

For those of you who are not familiar with them, the so-called 'Son of Sam' laws are a set of rulings that basically state that you, as an incarcerated felon, cannot make any money by selling your story or anything having to do with your criminal history; more broadly, some will say that you can't make money from books at all, even if they are entirely fictional.

The good news is, the Supreme Court ruled in 1991, in *Simon and Schuster v. Members of the New York State Crime Victims Board,* 502 U.S. 105 (1991) that the statute was unconstitutional in restricting free speech for two reasons.

The first was that it was being applied even if the author had not been accused or convicted, and applied to any work expressing the author's thoughts or memories of a crime. The First Amendment was cited as the basis for this part of the decision.

Second, the statute imposed a financial burden on individuals for the content of what they wanted to say, restricting income from an expressive activity while other income wasn't included.

So, the Son of Sam laws were thrown out in the highest court of our country. In addition to this, many states have also individually thrown the laws out over the years. This is not to say you will not encounter opposition, especially if you are writing about your criminal history; but it is not a complete brick wall at the federal level.

Chapter 27

Social Media

I'm sure you already know: social media is the big thing out here nowadays. If you don't have a social media presence your credibility drops quite a bit. Basically, everybody has one. That's a bit of an exaggeration, but not by much. And anyone who has a business (in your case, that business is writing books) pretty much needs one.

You have some choices on what social media platform you use, and the popular ones can wax and wane as the years go on. Currently the top options are Facebook, Twitter, and Instagram. Each of them has their own strengths and weaknesses. Facebook is pretty universal – it can be used for just about anyone, including authors. Twitter is pretty good as well, though it is a bit more limited for someone in prison. Instagram isn't really suited to promoting oneself as an author as it is mostly about photos (this is perhaps inaccurate if you are publishing an art book, I suppose). In addition to social media, there is the option to have a website, but I'll address that separately.

So, you should absolutely have a social media presence. Personally, I recommend Facebook, but Twitter is a close second. If you can do both, do so. But keep in mind that just having an account is not enough. Just like your book, if no one knows your social media account exists, they won't go to it. So you'll have to get the word out about your social media... but this can be easier than a full-scale marketing attempt for your book.

So, why do you need social media? Well, because 'all the cool kids are doing it', of course! And, though I say that in jest... it's not too far from the truth. First, people *expect* you to have something. As I mentioned before, if you have no social media presence, you instantly lose some credibility as a voice to be heard and listened to.

Second, it keeps your brand alive. This is probably the most important aspect of social media. All marketing needs to be steady and continuous. You can't just run one ad and expect it to be enough.

Consider Coca-Cola. You know what it is. You know where to get it. You know why you'd want it. They really don't need to build 'brand awareness', or inform you of their existence. And yet you still see their commercials – sometimes every day. Why? Well, there's a couple reasons. The first is that the commercial serves as a reminder. How often have you been watching TV, seen an ad for a food you like, and thought to yourself, "Man, that looks really good. I'd sure like to have one of those right now!" You already knew it existed, but the commercial made you think of it *right now*. And maybe *right now* is the moment you would actually go out and get one, whatever it was. You may have seen the ad last week, but you had just eaten, or you weren't in the mood for one, or whatever. But now… well, now, you just *have* to have one. So, your marketing isn't just out there to make people aware of what you're selling, it's to remind them of it at the right time, so that they go out and get it!

Second, many studies suggest that people are more likely to go out and buy something new only after they've seen an ad for it many times. So, you need to continue to put yourself (and your book) out there in the public's eye.

This goes for all advertising, but social media can be a great way to do it on the cheap. This does, of course, assume you have a following. But once you do, you need to maintain your activity. An idle Facebook or Twitter account does you no good. You need to be making posts on the regular. They can be just about anything, really… just keep it interesting enough that people don't put you on 'ignore'.

If you do your account as a personal account, you'll start connecting with old friends. Then you can branch out even further. However, you are trying to build a brand here, not just re-connect with your buddies from school. For this reason I always recommend building your author profile as well. This is set up more like a business page on Facebook, for example. You don't 'friend' people, but they can 'follow' your page. It has much the same result but has a few differences that I don't need to address here. I will mention one, though – you don't reach out to people like you do on a personal profile and have them 'friend' you. What you *can* do is request that people 'like' your page. This will automatically set them to 'follow' you, and they will see things you post from then on.

And what should you post? Well, as an author trying to build your brand and draw interest to your work, post as an author, as a business – not as Joe Smith, that guy you knew a few years back. Don't post memories of your trip to Mexico, or what you had for dinner last night. What you want to do is remember that this is a business. Post things that are relevant to that business. Post about writing (and this can cover a wide range of topics itself). Post about topics related to what your books are about. Post links to other pages or articles about writing or your books' topics.

Running a social media account is relatively easy to do from inside, so long as you have someone on the outside willing to put in a little bit of time here and there. You can write all your posts from where you sit and just have them put on your Facebook/Twitter/etc by your people, which only takes a couple minutes. You can even set up posts to only appear after a certain date, so your people can sit down for one hour and have posts set up to appear for the next six months.

You'll still want to monitor your account, responding to anyone commenting on what you have posted, etc. In addition, one way to gain more followers is to 'promote' a post. This is basically an advertisement. You take one post and set it to appear to people who fit a specific demographic. With any luck they will find the post interesting, check out your Facebook page, and 'like' it to continue seeing your new content.

Chapter 28

## Author Webpage

This one is not quite as necessary as it once was. You already have a few alternatives to this, most notably Amazon's Author Central and your social media options. So I won't spend too much time here.

If you have the resources it certainly doesn't hurt to have a webpage. You can use it as a blog, for one thing (if you have someone to upload your entries to it). What is a blog? Consider it a journal where you talk about whatever it is you want, at whatever length you want. Facebook/Twitter are a little too constrained for this sort of dissertation; it's not quite what they were made for. You really don't want your posts to be very long when posting to either of those sites – no one wants to read a 'wall of text' on social media. However, on your own website you can write as much as you like. Sometimes it can even be worth it to post up a whole short story. In fact, posting an entire short story can be useful to show people your writing style, or to keep people checking in on you and keep your name in their head. If they like this free option they are more likely to pick up a copy of your book. In a similar vein you can post up the first couple chapters here for free – again, if the visitor likes what they read, they are more likely to go out and buy the book (especially since you will have a very convenient link to the Amazon or Barnes & Noble page for your book here, or perhaps a way to buy it directly).

Having your own website gives you the flexibility that social media does not. And of course, you should have links from here to your social media accounts, just like you should have a link to your website from your social media accounts.

Again, you are here to promote your *book*, but this is a good place to put up a little more about yourself. People are often interested in the author of any book they like, and you have a more interesting story than most authors out here do… so use it! Put up a solid bio. Tell them about your interesting life. Obviously, you shouldn't brag about it – few people want to see an unrepentant convict – but they do love to hear the story of how you struggled, how you rose, how you fell, and how you are rising once again to be a better person than ever you were.

Of course, if your book is a memoir, don't tell them everything! Just enough to give them a taste of what they are in store for when they buy your book and read the *whole* story…

## Chapter 29

## Write More Books

This may be the most valuable chapter you will read. Why? Because I am about to MULTIPLY your earnings!

When you read a book you enjoy, are you simply done with it? Or do you wonder, "What else has this author written? I think I'm going to seek out more of their books."

If you don't ask yourself that question after a good book… I just don't know if I can even talk to you. The fact is, this is a question almost every reader considers when they've found a book they like. And then what happens? They buy more of that author's books. Which means this: However that author reached that reader in the first place, they have just DOUBLED the money they made from that reader. Oh, the author has ten books? Well then, instead of earning just

$5 from that one reader they have now earned $50. Math. Be cool, stay in school.

Let's say you spent $100 marketing your book. And let's also say that each book you sell brings you a profit of $1. And let's say that 100 people went out and bought your book. You just made your $100 back. Yippee.

Now let's say the above numbers are still true, but you have 5 books published. And they're good books. People who read one actually want to read more from you. So in this scenario each of those 100 people bought not just one of your books, but they bought all five of them. Now, instead of just making your $100 back, you have made $500. You're starting to make a profit. All without spending any additional money or time on marketing or promoting your book. It's true that some people have made a lot of money on just one book… but for 99% of all authors who are successful it's due in part to the fact that they have more than just one book out there. In fact, there is a group on Facebook for authors dedicated to making a living by just writing books. The group is called "20 Books to $50K." The concept is to get twenty good books out there, and with those twenty books to make $50,000 in one year. Why twenty books? Because even if each book does not sell amazingly well, with twenty of them you can get some good income brewing.

I worked with a lot of guys who would talk about how many books they had written, just waiting to publish. My advice to them was to *get those books out there*. All of them! Some wanted to see the first one succeed first. That's not the route to follow. Get those books out there. Get them out now. Why? Consider: one book alone may not make much of a splash – but a full series? Now you're selling! Also, people have short memories. They read your book and looked for more, but those other books haven't been published yet. Even if it's the first book of a series that hasn't released Part II yet, you may have lost a reader. A year from now when you get around to releasing Part II, is that reader going to be actually looking for it? They've moved on. You've got to get their attention all over again and *convince* them all over again. If the book is already out when they finish the first one, you've already got their attention, you've already got them hooked.

About fifteen years ago, I read a book series up to Book 11. ELEVEN thick-ass books. Literally thousands of pages. Books 12, 13, and 14 would finish the series, but they weren't out yet. Only now, FIFTEEN YEARS LATER, have I gotten back to the series, starting over from book one and working my way through. The author of the series actually died a few years back, so unfortunately isn't even able to enjoy the royalties my purchases would be putting in his pocket.

Moral of the story? Keep writing. Get those books out there, and get them sold before you can't enjoy the royalties anymore.

## Chapter 30

## Audiobooks

You may not have thought much about audiobooks since many of you don't have access to them (some of you may with your new tablets). Audiobooks are an absolutely under-utilized way to get your book to more people. They are also, however, fairly costly for most.

With the advent of easily accessed and transported digital media, audiobooks have really been making a strong venture into many book-lovers' libraries. People can easily load them up on their phone or tablet and listen to their favorite books while they do... pretty much anything. I know people who listen to books while they're cooking, driving, working out, working at their job... really, just about anything.

But while the big publishers have started to really push this niche, very few of the smaller, newer authors are really getting their stuff put out on this medium. And that means that when you do so, you have MUCH LESS competition than you do for the print or digital format of your book. People simply have fewer options for books to listen to, so they are much more likely to come across and listen to yours.

    The problem, as mentioned, is that this option can be fairly pricey – enough to put it out of reach for most incarcerated authors. If you have a shorter book, that can help since you are typically paying per word or per hour for the voice professional to record your book. You may be tempted to just go cheap and have your buddy on the street record it for you, but I would advise against it. You want your book to be well-represented by someone who knows how to not just read well but who can speak your words smoothly as they read, with proper inflections, recorded on professional level equipment, who understands proper vocal pacing, and so much more. You don't want your book printed in crayon, do you? Don't have an amateur record your passion. Hmmm… that may have come out wrong. Get your mind out of the gutter.

CHAPTER 31

BOOK REVIEWS

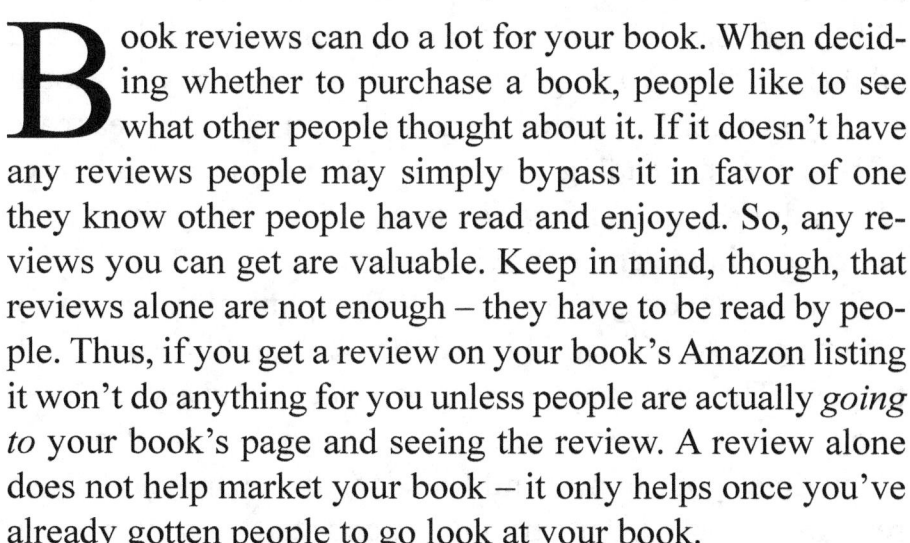

Book reviews can do a lot for your book. When deciding whether to purchase a book, people like to see what other people thought about it. If it doesn't have any reviews people may simply bypass it in favor of one they know other people have read and enjoyed. So, any reviews you can get are valuable. Keep in mind, though, that reviews alone are not enough – they have to be read by people. Thus, if you get a review on your book's Amazon listing it won't do anything for you unless people are actually *going to* your book's page and seeing the review. A review alone does not help market your book – it only helps once you've already gotten people to go look at your book.

Some reviews, like those made by Clarion, Blue Ink, etc, are automatically posted and made available to people who follow their reviews. While services like these carry a premium charge (several hundred for a single review!), you can also look at it as free marketing beyond the review itself, since the review will be posted where people will read it. So not only is it a review, it is an actual ad for you book as well.

However, when most people think of book reviews they are thinking of reviews posted by other readers on Amazon, Barnes & Noble, Goodreads, or any of those sites. You can be sure that these reviews are very valuable. Many authors view them as worth their weight in gold (although they are digital, so weigh nothing… maybe not the best metaphor). There are many different websites where you can go to get reviews. This is done in many ways – sometimes by simply exchanging reviews in a 'you scratch my back, I'll scratch yours" sort of arrangement, where an author will read your book and review it and you do the same for them. There are even people who you can pay to leave a review for you. Most of these places of any sort are fraught with legal and ethical questions. The general consensus is that you should not pay someone to write a review for you as it is a clear case of bias and misleading to the consumer. Amazon in particular is diligent in hunting down any review they feel might not be legitimate and removing them.

So how do you get reviews? Well, organically is one way – some people will simply read the book and like it enough to post. This will happen maybe once for every hundred books you sell. Yeah, it's that rare. As you are starting out, many times your family and friends will be happy to leave a review for you. This is certainly a good start. It is even worth encouraging everyone you interact with to not just read your book but to leave a review, especially on Amazon.

A final note on reviews: if you get a bad one, DO NOT ENGAGE. Don't try to argue with whoever left the bad review (you can reply to reviews on most sites). This typically degenerates into a childish bickering and does not do you any favors. Just ignore it and move on, get some more good reviews to compensate for that one bad review.

Finally, how about Book Bloggers? What *is* a book blogger, you ask? I'm sure you've heard of "Influencers" – people who have a following on social media who can get a product to sell just by using and recommending it themselves? Well, book bloggers are the same thing, just for books.

Basically, the way it works is pretty straightforward. The blogger reads a book, then writes (or talks, or videos) about it on their blog or whatever platform they use. Their followers then will often listen to their recommendations and pick up whatever book they recommended. This can be a very powerful and effective marketing tool.

Of course, it's not as easy as all that. Actually, it is, but the problem is that the popular book bloggers are already so booked up (see what I did there? Booked up? Get it? I should write comedy)... where was I? Ah yes, the popular book bloggers are so booked up they have no time to accept your book. They already have every author offering their book to them. And if they do accept your book expect that it will be a few months before they get to it, at best.

But it is still a viable, inexpensive option. You will need outside help to find the bloggers, but we'll assume you have that.

But don't waste your – or the bloggers – time. Be sure the blogger you're approaching reads books of your genre. Don't waste everyone's time asking them to read your sci-fi book when they only read westerns. When reaching out to them, they want to know about your book, and maybe a little bit about you as well. Many will have a form on their website to fill out for book submissions. Be sure to give them all the information they need (they often want word or page count, genre, title, a link to the book on Amazon, and a brief synopsis). Be sure to offer it in whatever format they prefer: paperback, digital, etc.

## Afterward

Well, that's it! At least for now, until I release Part II which will cover... Frankly, I have no idea what it would cover – I've squeezed it all into here!

Following is a couple appendices with examples, web sites, stuff like that. But hopefully you now have a new trove of knowledge and ideas you can build on to bring success to your own book (actually, your own BOOKS – remember the chapter on writing more books!). I would genuinely love to hear from you about your experiences – successful and otherwise - and perhaps even if you have some ideas or resources you think I should have included but did not! You can reach me via snail mail at:

Francis Raemond
c/o Cadmus Publishing
PO Box 2146
Port Angeles, WA 98362

You can also find more at my website: www.inmatebookmarketing.com. There are a bunch of links and useful things there.

Finally, I can't recommend my publisher, Cadmus Publishing, enough. As mentioned, I used to work there myself and they do their best to do everything they can to help you, the incarcerated author, succeed. Not only do they publish books from inmates, they can help you edit, market, type, pretty much everything you need, from start to finish. Even if you plan to publish on your own or through another publisher, you can still avail yourself of many of their services.

Good luck, and keep writing!

Frank Raemond
Washington State, 2022

## Appendix A: Resources

In almost all categories, there are simply too many options to list. And some of them may not work well with incarcerated authors, or they may have changed their policies since I last dealt with them for my incarcerated clients. I'll put a couple of the big ones up here. Please feel free to drop me a note and let me know if you have any input – like if you know a good option for inmates, or if you have reached out to the people below, how was your experience, etc, so I can include any changes in any future updates! (currently November, 2022)

**Editing**
https://aceseditors.org/resources/for-hire
    Nothing of note – just a good site to find editors.
Fiverr – fiverr.com
    Really, this place has a lot of options for different things: editors, artists, etc.
Cadmus Publishing – cadmuspublishing.com
    Specifically, you will want to reach out to the Author Liaison who works specifically with incarcerated authors. You can reach that person at info@cadmus-publishing.com (they will route the email to the right person), or 360-565-6459 (this is the number straight to the Author Liaison desk, so that they can accept prison phone calls).

**Typing**

Cadmus Publishing – cadmuspublishing.com

Specifically, you will want to reach out to the Author Liaison who works specifically with incarcerated authors. You can reach that person at info@cadmus-publishing.com (they will route the email to the right person), or 360-565-6459 (this is the number straight to the Author Liaison desk, so that they can accept prison phone calls).

Ambler Document Processing

No known website. You will be working with Jane Eichwold, who works with a lot of incarcerated authors. You can email her at jane@protypeexpress.com

**Beta Readers**

Goodreads beta reader group - https://www.goodreads.com/group/show/50920-beta-reader-group

A great free resource for finding beta readers of all types. Be sure to read the rules of the group and understand what is required and what you are looking for. A huge help for your first time looking for a beta reader.

Betareader.io - https://betareader.io/

If you want to work with a company specializing in Beta Readers, this is probably the best one out there. Be prepared for more fees than finding them yourself, though.

**Publishing**

Cadmus Publishing – cadmuspublishing.com

Specifically, you will want to reach out to the Author Liaison who works specifically with incarcerated authors. You can reach that person at info@cadmus-publishing.com (they will route the email to the right person), or 360-565-6459 (this is the number straight to the Author Liaison desk, so that they can accept prison phone calls).

Word Out Books – https://www.windinghall.com/word-outbooks

This division of Winding Hall is set up specifically for incarcerated authors. However, as of this writing, they are not accepting new submissions until Summer of 2023.

Reedsy – reedsy.com

Book Baby – bookbaby.com

**Promotions**

Book Bub – bookbub.com

For readers, BookBub is a free service that helps millions of readers discover books they'll love while providing publishers and authors with a way to drive sales and find new fans. As an author, you can submit your book with a special deal (like $0.99 for the epub) for a limited time for BookBub readers to take advantage of. Not all publishers allow this because they still have to cover their costs (for example, I know Cadmus does not, and I believe the same can be said for Word Out Books) – but if you completely self-publish, then it can be a good option.

Booky Call – bookycall.com

It's like Tinder, but for books. It's a bit off-beat, but if you wanna try something different... Basically, a reader puts in their preferences, and then they can 'swipe right' on books they're interested in. Books are presented as though they were a potential date, with ideas for date night with the book, what the book is into, etc. Cute.

**Marketing**

Really, there are too many options for marketing service providers to list. And to be frank, I haven't tried all of them out for whether they will work with incarcerated authors. I'll put a couple of the big ones up here. Let me know if you have any input – like if you reach out to them, how was your experience, etc, so I can include any changes in any future updates!

Cadmus Publishing – cadmuspublishing.com
Elite Authors Marketing - Eliteauthors.com
Smith Publicity - smithpublicity.com
Book Marketeers - bookmarketeers.com

**Interviews/journalists**

RadioGuestList.com

This place has a free subscription you can get in your email every week (normal email only, not prison email systems) that will tell you about places that are looking for a specific type of person to interview. As the name implies, this is almost always for radio interviews, though they also do a few podcasts and the like. If you get a paid subscription (which is pretty cheap) you get even more emails with more opportunities. Cadmus has had a lot of success with this group.

HARO (Help A Reporter Out) – helpareporter.com
This is a bit more difficult to navigate – your people on the outside will be doing much of this work for you, but it is a great resource if you have the right people.

**Press Release**

All of these do basically the same thing. At Cadmus (when I was there) we used Newswire, but I don't think there's really much difference between any of them besides cost.

PRNewswire.com
Newswire.com
Cision.com
Einpresswire.com

**Genre Research**

Amazon.com (just look at sales numbers for the different genres to get a feel for them)
Authorearnings.com
thecreativepenn.com/genre

# Appendix B: Sample Press Releases

This is a Press Release released by Cadmus Publishing for one of their incarcerated authors, and is a fine example you can take as an idea of how to lay your own out. I'll highlight my comments throughout it in bracketed *<bold italics>*.

## Sample Press Release 1

*<This first paragraph should provide an introduction – just as in pretty much anything else. The most basic and important points should be found here. If a person reads just the first paragraph, they should have a pretty good idea what the whole thing is about, and grab their attention for more.>* A stunning tell-all book about prison life, mass incarceration, and how society creates and confines its most vulnerable populations, *Living in Reality: Everything I Needed to Know I Learned in Prison* is a stark look at the U.S. prison system, with insider perspective from David W. Jones who experiences it first-hand as an incarcerated inmate.

David W. Jones, a.k.a. "DJ", experienced every bump the road threw at him, eventually leading him to his life as an inmate currently confined in a Texas prison. Upon his incarceration, he learned that the U.S. Federal Prison System is not in the business of "rehabilitation," but instead exacerbates criminal behaviors. DJ's story of survival, *Living in Reality: Everything I Needed to Know I Learned in Prison*, touches not only on the day-to-day dealings of the prison system, but also acts as a warning for parents and teachers about the criminal mindset that they could be instilling in their children.

*<A good PR will have at least one quote from the author, possibly more. People want to read about something interesting, generally about you the author or what led you to write this particular book. A PR is NOT just something to say, "I wrote a book about X; go buy it!" You need to grab their interest, and people are interested in people.>*
"If you want to know about a society, look at their prisons." Addressing current hot-button issues, including racism, the #MeToo movement, and ex post facto laws, DJ encourages us to examine the fine line between society and prison that may not be as fine as we think.

*<The next two sections give some specific information with a heading (The Book and About the author). Though this is not necessary, Cadmus often uses this method to break things up for people interested in those items specifically.>* **The book:** *Living in Reality: Everything I Needed to Know I Learned in Prison* is for anyone who wonders, "What's really going on?" Sharing his first-hand knowledge gained as an incarcerated inmate, David W. Jones uses the story of his childhood and his insights into the justice system to explain how the U.S. government is not actually invested in the rehabilitation of criminals. He offers his unique perspective to parents, teachers, and society at large to show that prison is not that far off from reality as we know it.

**About the author:** *<People want to know about you. Give some interesting details here. Consider the factors discussed earlier in this book about what will help you to sell it – do you divulge case history? Do you just focus on*

*how far you've come? Do you talk about why you were injustly locked up? There is no one good answer – you will have to decide for yourself.>* David W. Jones, a.k.a. DJ, has been an inmate in the state of Texas for 30 years. His time incarcerated has changed him in many ways, despite the prison's anti-rehabilitation practices, and he believes that society needs to start living in reality, not hiding from it.

*<Don't forget to give the information people need to get the book or contact you. That's the whole point of this, after all! Typically this will go at the very end.>* Living in Reality: Everything I Needed to Know I Learned in Prison is available from all major online book retailers. For more information, please visit the author's website at www.davidwjones71.com or contact **Cadmus Publishing** at **info@cadmuspublishing.com**.

## Sample Press Release 2

This new collection of poems and prose released by Word Out Books is a gift from its author to the creators of humankind: women. In Wild Roses, Stanley Corbett Jr. "Knowledge G" honors the strength of the original women, recognizing that they are the powerful foundation upon which society is built. Within these pages, the reader will be taken on a journey of love for the spirit of the divine Feminine.

Wild Roses is an homage to the author's love and respect for womankind. This book was written for your mother, your grandmother, your wife, or for anyone that admires the spirit of women and their odyssey through time.

About the Author: Stanley Earl Corbett Jr. was born and raised in Lexington, NC. Incarcerated since age 19, he has discovered writing and poetry as an outlet during this confinement. He has authored another publication "The Heart & Soul of a Poet" and is a proud member of the National Writers Association.

Currently, Corbett is housed at Central Prison in Raleigh, NC and is a passionate proponent of human rights. He is proud to be a part of the group "Incarcerated Workers Organizing Committee" (IWOC)- which advocates for the civil rights of prisoners throughout the United States. In concurrence with IWOC, he also participates in the groups "Prison Lives Matter" and "NC-CURE." Corbett's goal is to remind society that inmates are human beings and their accomplishments deserve to be shared with the world: "There's plenty of stories in the media concerning prisoners swindling the IRS to receive additional stimulus checks. Where's the positive stories?" He utilized his own stimulus check to aid in publishing his poetry; that is the kind of story he wishes to share! You can purchase copies of "Wild Roses" on amazon.com or wordoutbooks.com. You can also access "The Heart and Soul of a Poet" by searching Stanley Corbett on prisonsfoundation.org.

## APPENDIX C: ABOUT THE AUTHOR

Look, you already read about me in Part I, Chapter 2. And if you didn't, go back and read it! Besides what I already said there, I live with my wife in the Pacific Northwest, where the mountains meet the ocean – one of the most beautiful parts of the country. I grew up in the Midwest, so I appreciate the mild weather we found out here (if you've ever lived in Michigan or Minnesota or Wisconsin... you'll know what I mean - too hot in the summer, too cold in the winter!!!). I am a child of the 80s, and have spent most of my life working in the book industry in some fashion or another. If you want to know more... well, why? Are you stalking me? 😊

I'd love to hear from you. You can reach me through Cadmus Publishing, since they published this book!

Francis Raemond
c/o Cadmus Publishing
PO Box 2146
Port Angeles, WA 98362

www.ingramcontent.com/pod-product-compliance
Lightning Source LLC
Chambersburg PA
CBHW071859070526
44583CB00016B/1763